ANSWERS FOR
DIFFICULT DAYS

SURVIVING THE STORM OF SECULARISM

by David Quine

Seven Studies from the Word of God

Cover Masterpiece:
Ludolf Backhuysen, 1631-1708
Detail of:
Ships in Distress off a Rocky Coast (1667)
Photograph © Board of Trustees
Oil on canvas, 45 x 65 7/8 in
Ailsa Mellon Bruce Fund
National Gallery of Art
Washington D.C.

Answers for Difficult Days
is from the Introduction to
World Views to the Western World Volume II
David Quine © 1998

Published by:
The Cornerstone Curriculum Project
2006 Flat Creek Place
Richardson, Texas 75080

CONTENTS

Answers for Difficult Days

Surviving the Storm of Secularism

In today's culture there is a constant battle of ideas. The secularization of our culture is rapidly approaching completion. We must heed the Apostle Paul's warning. "We are no longer to be children, tossed here and there by waves, and carried about by every wind of doctrine, by the trickery of men, by craftiness in deceitful scheming: but speaking the truth in love" (Eph.4:14).

The picture Paul paints is of children in a boat being hopelessly tossed to and fro between gusts of teaching of opposing philosophies, cleverly disguised lies made to sound like truth.

These basic Bible studies are intended to give a broad understanding of the Biblical world view. Though not exhaustive, this study forms the basis of standing free from the thoughts and ideas of the secular culture.

7 Vital Questions

To use the Biblical world view as the standard for making personal decisions and evaluating others thoughts and ideas we must thoroughly know the Scriptural answers to these seven vital questions. Then as we read an essay or novel, listen to a political speech, observe a series of paintings, or watch a movie we can measure these works against the Biblical world view to determine if what is being said is true or false. To understand or appreciate is important, but to discern truth (to evaluate) is vital if we are to successfully ride the storm of secularism!

- Is there a God or gods? If so, what is He like?
- What is the nature of the universe — its origin?
- What is the essential nature of man?
- What is the basis of ethics and morality?
- What is the cause of evil and suffering?
- What happens to man at death?
- What is the meaning of history?

These are the important questions we answer as we build our own personal world view. The best way to use this study is to look up each passage, read the verses carefully, make several observations, and then write a statement that explains what it means.

Study Number 1

WHO OR WHAT

WAS BEFORE THE BEGINNING?

Is there a God? If so, What is He like?

"In the beginning God …"

Genesis 1:1

"For the wrath of God is revealed from heaven against all ungodliness and unrighteousness of men who suppress the truth in unrighteousness, because that which is known about God is evident within them; for God made it evident to them. For since the creation of the world His invisible attributes, His eternal power and divine nature, have been clearly seen, being understood through what has been made, so that they are without excuse."

Romans 1:18-20

There are several lines of reasoning that can be used to talk with someone regarding the existence of God: The universe and its form, and man.

THE UNIVERSE • Cause and Effect
We are surrounded by a 'cause and effect' world. Everything that a person does has some effect. When it comes to the origin of the universe there are only two choices. One belief is that nothing caused this world; however, an effect without a cause has never been observed to happen. The second belief is that something caused this world. This 'something' may be natural selection, or one might conclude that God was the cause.

"Our wisdom, if it is to be thought genuine, consists almost entirely of two parts, the knowledge of God and of ourselves."

John Calvin

"The Bible gives us the explanation for the existence of the universe and for the mannishness of man. Or, to reverse this, … the universe and its form and the mannishness of man are a testimony to the truth of the Bible."

Francis Schaeffer

THE UNIVERSE • Intelligent Design

The world in which we live is a world that seems to have a purpose. How is this best explained? Is this world a system of intricate patterns or is there just an illusion of patterns? The nontheist explains that the universe happened by chance through the process of natural selection. The question remains, however: Can random 'by chance' actions result in the highly integrated organization which is evident in the world about us?

MAN • THE UNIQUENESS OF MAN

How can the uniqueness of man be explained? How can man's moral nature, his intelligence, and mental abilities be accounted for? The answer given by modern man is that all of this evolved. The biologist and social scientist have proposed very elaborate explanations of how this has happened. The biologist considers man only as a biological or organic animal. The sociologist explains man as a cultural creature. Both the biologist and the sociologist rely upon chance as the mechanism to produce such a creature. But does this explain conscience or that reaching out for a belief in a higher being which seems to be universal to every culture? Or does the uniqueness of man point to the existence of a personal God?

READ THESE PASSAGES   WHAT DO THESE PASSAGES SAY ABOUT GOD?

    Deuteronomy 6:4
    James 2:19

READ THESE PASSAGES   WHAT DO THESE PASSAGES SAY ABOUT GOD?

    Genesis 1:26
    Genesis 11:7
    Isaiah 6:8
    Matthew 3:16,17
    John 15:26
    I Peter 1:2

READ THESE PASSAGES   WHAT DO THESE PASSAGES SAY ABOUT GOD?

    Ephesians 4:5
    Matthew 28:19

Since there is one baptism and since there is one God, who has been revealed as the Father, the Son and the Holy Spirit, therefore the three persons, by whom God is known, coexist.

READ THESE PASSAGES   WHAT DO THESE PASSAGES SAY ABOUT GOD?

Genesis 1:1, 31
Psalms 33:9
Isaiah 44:24
Isaiah 45:18
John 1: 1-3
Colossians 1:16,17
Hebrews 11:3
Revelation 4:11

READ THESE PASSAGES   WHAT DO THESE PASSAGES SAY ABOUT GOD?

Nehemiah 9:6
Psalms 36:6,7
Psalms 107:9
Psalms 121:8
Hebrews 1:3

READ THESE PASSAGES   WHAT DO THESE PASSAGES SAY ABOUT GOD?

I Chronicles 29:11,12
Psalms 66:7
Isaiah 45:7
Daniel 4:35
Romans 11:36
Ephesians 1:11
Revelation 19:6

READ THESE PASSAGES   WHAT DO THESE PASSAGES SAY ABOUT GOD?

Matthew 6:26
Matthew 10:29
I Peter 5:6,7

A Mighty Fortress Is Our God
Martin Luther

A mighty Fortress is our God, A bulwark never failing,
Our helper He amid the flood Of mortal ills prevailing.
For still our ancient foe Doth seek to work us woe —
His craft and power are great,
    And, armed with cruel hate,
On earth is not His equal.

Did we in our own strength confide,
    Our striving would be losing.
Were not the right man on our side,
    The man of God's own choosing.
Dost ask who that may be? Christ Jesus, it is He —
Lord Sabaoth is His name, From age to age the same,
And He must win the battle.

And though this world with devils filled,
    Should threaten to undo us,
We will not fear,
for God hath willed His truth to triumph through us,
The prince of darkness grim, We tremble not for him-
His rage we can endure, For lo, his doom is sure:
One little word shall fell him.

That word above all earthly powers,
    No thanks to them, abideth;
The Spirit and the gifts are ours through Him
    who with us sideth.
Let goods and kindred go, This mortal life also —
The body they may kill, God's truth abideth still:
His kingdom is forever.

"After realizing that there is a Creator, [faith] must then infer that He is also Governor and Preserver, not just because He can produce a kind of general motion in the machine of the universe, as well as in each of its parts, but because by His special Providence He sustains and cares for everything He has made down to the smallest sparrow!"

The Institutes of Christian Religion, John Calvin

Summarize your thoughts about the nature and character of God. Include any key verses.
Select one or more verses to memorize.

_____
_____
_____
_____
_____
_____
_____
_____
_____
_____
_____
_____
_____
_____
_____
_____
_____
_____
_____
_____
_____
_____
_____
_____
_____
_____
_____
_____
_____
_____
_____
_____
_____
_____
_____

Study Number 2

THE UNIVERSE

What is the origin of the universe?

Genesis chapters 1 and 2, and chapter 5 verses 1 and 2.
Circle the word 'created' in these passages

Write or draw what happened on each day.

Genesis 1:1
In the beginning God created the heavens and the earth.

"The world 'create' used here means to create out of nothing.
God created matter out of nothing. He did not just shape
preexistent matter but brought it into being. He did not make
only the world, but the heavens and the earth — everything
there is. He created all things out of nothing. They now have
objective existence; they are not an extension of Himself or His
essence."

Francis Schaeffer,
<u>25 Basic Bible Studies</u>

Read Psalms 33:6, 9

Write a paragraph summarizing what these passages say about the universe.

_____
_____
_____
_____

Using your Bible concordance find at least 10 other passages that refer to the origin of the world.

_____
_____
_____
_____
_____
_____
_____
_____
_____
_____
_____
_____
_____
_____
_____
_____
_____
_____
_____
_____
_____
_____
_____
_____

Study Number 3

MAN

What is the nature of man - what is he like?

MAN
We learn from Genesis that God created man from the dust of the ground. But we are also told that God breathed life into Adam to make him a living person. The ground made up the material while the life of God made up the immaterial. Though we think of man as consisting of two parts, a material part and an immaterial, man is a unity. The immaterial was never intended to be separated from the material. Together they compose the whole man.

THE MATERIAL
The body is described in II Corinthians 5:1 as our 'earthly house,' our temporary dwelling place. The material part of man is quite diverse: consisting of arms, legs, blood vessels, etc.

THE IMMATERIAL
The immaterial portion of man is described by a variety of words in the Bible. These words include soul, spirit, heart, will, etc.

According to John Calvin '...the soul consists of two parts, the intellect and the will." The heart is thought to be the seat of our emotions. The immaterial portion of man allows him to react mentally, emotionally, and volitionally within the 'capacity limits' with which each has been endowed by the Creator.

"You behave by the exercise of your will under the influence of your mind and your emotions, and this process does not in itself require any visible activity on the part of the body. Your body is required only when you wish to give outward expression to your inward behavior — in other words, when you wish to communicate with your external circumstances, and the way in which you ultimately communicate by physical activity may far from represent your true internal behavior! 'The words of his mouth were smoother than butter [external behavior], but war was in his heart [internal behavior]: his words were softer than oil, yet were they drawn swords' (Ps. 55:21)." — Ian Thomas

There is a children's book that asks this question:

What makes a bird a bird?

Of course several ideas may come to mind. For example, flying...wings...nests...eggs. Though birds do fly, so do butterflies. That is not what distinguishes a bird from other created life. Yes, birds have wings, but so do flies. Although many birds do lay eggs in nests, so do some snakes. What makes a bird a bird? Feathers!

What about man? What makes man a man? Is it his body? We need to know why we consider ourselves to be men as distinct from mere animals and not just animals that happen to be called men. This is a very critical question for 20th century man and will continue to be so for the 21st century!

Dr. Schaeffer has drawn the following diagram to illustrate the similarities between man, animals, plants, and machines as well as to clarify the difference between them:

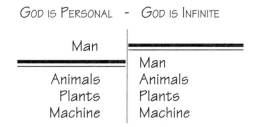

GOD IS PERSONAL - GOD IS INFINITE

Man	
Animals	Man
Plants	Animals
Machine	Plants
	Machine

Man is distinct from animals, plants, and the machine part of creation because man, like God, is personal. However, man is like animals, plants, and the machine portion of the creation in that we are all finite.

"What is the essential difference between man as God intended and the rest of the animal kingdom? God has given to man what He has not given to any other form of created life - the human spirit... intrinsically indivisible from the human soul. As the marrow within the joints, so is the human spirit buried deep within the human soul, remaining essentially distinct, yet together forming that complete immaterial entity capable of endless survival after physical death, as opposed to the purely 'animal soul' common to the rest of the animal kingdom, which possesses no such capacity either to survive or to be held morally responsible beyond the grave." — Ian Thomas

Read I Timothy 6:13-16, Hebrews 9:14 and John 5:26.
What do these passages teach about God and man?

_____

_____

_____

_____

_____

"It is for this reason that God is absolute, self-sufficient, and completely independent. All other forms of life — vegetable, animal, spiritual or angelic — are essentially 'created' and not 'self-existent' and remain dependent upon the Creator as the one who is the only source and sustainer of all life." —
Ian Thomas

Read Acts 17:24-25, 28; Job 12:10; Daniel 5:23

What ideas do these passages add to our understanding of the nature of God and His creation?

_____

_____

_____

_____

_____

_____

Use a dictionary to look up the word 'Immortality'.

_____

_____

_____

_____

_____

Read II Timothy 1:10.
What ideas come to light with this passage?

_____

_____

_____

"The human spirit is this unique capacity which God has given to man, which enables him both to receive and be motivated by the very life of God Himself. ['The spirit of man is the candle of the Lord' (Prov. 20:27a)] ...the human spirit is the lamp, incapable itself of producing light, but capable of receiving that which working in and through it produces light, and upon which it must be constantly dependent if it is to fulfill the purpose for which, as a lamp, it was created.

"As translated in Proverbs 20:20, the word 'candle' means lamp, and what electricity is to an electric lamp and what oil is to an oil lamp, the Holy Spirit is to the human spirit. With relentless consistency throughout the Scriptures, oil represents the person and office of the Holy Spirit, in whose person God is able to inhabit man's humanity and make him a partaker of His own divine nature, whereby man may be not only physically alive, as an animal, but spiritually alive, like God (II Peter 1:3-4). — Ian Thomas

Read Isaiah 57:15; II Peter 1:4.
What do you learn about man's relationship to God from these passages?

_____
_____
_____
_____
_____
_____

"It is your capacity to receive God, to enjoy God, and to be enjoyed by God which makes you man as opposed to mere animal, and it is only God in you that enables you to function as He intended you as man to function.

"Lose God, and lose everything that truly makes you man and enables you to behave as God intended man to behave! The anarchy of godlessness begins! The human spirit destitute of the Holy Spirit leaves the soul abandoned as a ship without a rudder on a storm-tossed sea, spiritually bankrupt, dead — 'alienated from the life of God' (Ephesians 4:18) — an easy prey to every evil, malicious, and malevolent influence of which it my fall foul!"

The Mystery of Godliness, Ian Thomas

THE FIRST ADAM

THE FIRST MAN — ADAM — AS HE WAS CREATED TO BE

READ THESE PASSAGES   THESE PASSAGES TEACH MAN AS:

Genesis 1:26-2:3   _____
Genesis 5:1-2   _____

Three phrases stand out regarding the nature of man:

- made in the likeness of God • good • very good

• What does 'created in the image of God' mean to you?

• If you could have looked at Adam in his relationship with Eve, or the creation, what would you have seen?

Adam was created so that he could bear the image of God without God becoming visible. It was through Adam and Eve and their descendants that the very image of God was to be made visible. God's nature and character was to be flowing from man — not because they were trying to imitate God, but rather because God Himself was living in and through Adam. Adam and Eve were alive spiritually!

In these opening verses we find Adam, made in the 'image of God,' spiritually alive, in a perfect environment, with a wonderful wife and a personal relationship with God — in which they walked together. Man was in harmony with the whole of creation — "it was very good." What happened? To look at man's behavior today one would certainly wonder about the 'image of God' in man.

THE FIRST MAN — ADAM — AS HE NOW IS

READ THESE PASSAGES

Genesis 3

- What is the significance of the forbidden fruit?

- What had God said to Adam about eating the fruit? (Genesis 2:17)

- How was Adam to affirm both his desire to please God and at the same time acknowledge that his very life depended on God?

- What was the deception of Satan?

- Although God said that Adam would die in the day that he ate of the forbidden fruit, the Bible says that Adam lived 930 years and then died. What happened to Adam that eventful day? What were the consequences of this historic event for Adam and Eve? … for the rest of mankind?

• Adam was created in the 'image of God.' However, after the fall of man we read that Adam became the father of a son 'in his own likeness, according to his image.' The whole human race has been born 'in Adam' — in the marred image of ungodlike behavior patterns. The human race is the antithesis of what we were created to be!

READ THESE PASSAGES

Ephesians 2:1; 4:18   In Adam you are ...

Romans 3:10-18   In Adam you walk ...
Ephesians 2:2-3
Colossians 1:21

John 8:24   In Adam you will ...

• Describe mankind 'in Adam'.

_____
_____
_____
_____
_____
_____
_____
_____

• Why is our culture particularly intent upon discrediting Adam and Eve as historic people?

_____
_____
_____
_____
_____
_____
_____
_____
_____
_____
_____
_____
_____
_____
_____
_____
_____
_____
_____
_____
_____
_____
_____
_____
_____
_____
_____
_____
_____
_____
_____
_____

THE LAST ADAM

Who is Jesus Christ?

THE LAST ADAM

READ THESE PASSAGES   JESUS IS ...

Romans 5:12-21
I Corinthians 15:20-24, 45-48   _____

_____

_____

_____

_____

_____

READ THESE PASSAGES   JESUS IS ...

I Timothy 3:16   _____
I Timothy 2:5, 6   _____
Hebrews 2:14   _____
Hebrews 9:15; 12:24   _____

                                _____

                                _____

_____

_____

• Why would you say that Jesus is the only person quali-
fied as this mediator?

_____

_____

_____

_____

_____

READ THESE PASSAGES   JESUS IS ...

Isaiah 7:14   _____
Galatians 4:4   _____
Genesis 3:15   _____
Luke 1:27-38   _____
Matthew 1:18-25   _____

_____
_____
_____

• Why is the virgin birth so important to Christianity?

_____
_____
_____
_____
_____

READ THESE PASSAGES   JESUS IS ...

Deuteronomy 18:15,18 _____
John 1:18   _____
John 1:1,2   _____
Colossians 2:9   _____
I John 5:20   _____
John 14:26; 16:12-14 _____

_____
_____
_____

READ THESE PASSAGES   JESUS IS ...

Psalms 110:4   _____
Mark 10:45   _____
John 1:29   _____
I Corinthians 5:7   _____
Exodus 12   _____
Ephesians 5:2   _____
Hebrews 3:1   _____
Hebrews 4:14; 6:20   _____
Hebrews 5:5,6   _____

Hebrews 7:26,27 _____

Hebrews 8:1 _____

Hebrews 9:25-28 _____

Hebrews 10:11-14 _____

Hebrews 10: 19-22 _____

_____

I Peter 3:18 _____

I John 4:10 _____

I John 2:1 _____

Hebrews 9:24 _____

John 17:9 _____

John 17:20 _____

Romans 8:34 _____

_____

_____

_____

_____

_____

READ THESE PASSAGES   JESUS IS ...

Genesis 49:10 _____

II Samuel 7:16 _____

Matthew 1:1; 22:42 _____

Psalms 2:6 _____

Isaiah 9:6,7 _____

Micah 5:2 _____

Luke 1:31-33 _____

Matthew 2:2 _____

John 1:49 _____

Luke 19:37,38 _____

John 18:37 _____

John 19:2, 3, 12, 14, _____

15, 19, 21, 22 _____

Acts 17:7 _____

_____

_____

_____

_____

Matthew 28:18
Ephesians 1:20-22
_____
_____

Hebrews 2:8
Acts 1:6,7
I Timothy 6:14,15
Matthew 25:31-34
Revelation 17:14; 19:16
_____
_____
_____
_____
_____

Colossians 1:13
Ephesians 5:23,24
Luke 19:11-27
_____
_____
_____
_____

_____
_____
_____
_____
_____

- Compare and contrast the first and second Adam.

_____
_____
_____
_____
_____
_____
_____
_____
_____
_____
_____
_____
_____
_____
_____
_____
_____
_____

SALVATION from the

Penalty ... Power ... Presence of Sin

READ THESE PASSAGES   SALVATION IS ...

John 3:15, 16, 18
John 3:36
Romans 3:9-20
Isaiah 64:6
Galatians 3:24
Romans 2:1-3
Acts 16:30-33
Romans 4:9-11
Romans 9:6
Romans 9:30-33
Galatians 2:16
Romans 3:21-26
John 8:24
John 14:6
Acts 4:12

"As the word 'salvation' is used here and throughout the New Testament, it has a much wider meaning than is usually given to it today. Today it is often limited to becoming a Christian. The scriptural use of the term includes all those things in the past, present, and future that will come to the man or woman who has accepted Christ as his or her Savior."

Dr. Francis Schaeffer,
25 Basic Bible Studies.

Romans 1:16
Romans 3:20
James 2:10
Romans 4:1-9, 22-25
Romans 5:1
Colossians 2:13,14
Isaiah 38:17; 43:25
Micah 7:19
Isaiah 53:4,5
Romans 5:8,9
Acts 13,38,39
Romans 3:28
Galatians 2:16

_____

What is justification and how is it related to salvation?

_____

Romans 6
Romans 7
Romans 8
Colossians 3;1-3
John 15:1-5
I Thessalonians 5:23
Hebrews 13:20,21
Ephesians 5:25, 26
Titus 2:11-14
Galatians 5:16-25
Ephesians 5:18; 4:30
I Thessalonians 5:19
Ephesians 3:14-19
II Corinthians 12:9
I John 5:3-5

_____
_____
_____
_____
_____
_____
_____
_____
_____
_____
_____
_____
_____
_____

"We have seen that once we accept Christ as Savior, we are justified....While justification deals with the past (once I have become a Christian), sanctification deals with the present. It has to do with the power of sin in the Christian's life. Justification is the same for all Christians, but obviously sanctification has proceeded further in some Christians than in others. For a book-length study of the subject of sanctification, [read] TRUE SPIRITUALITY."

Dr. Francis Schaeffer,
25 Basic Bible Studies.

"Now to Him Who is able to keep you without stumbling, or slipping, or falling and to present [you] unblemished (blameless and faultless) before the presence of His glory — with unspeakable, ecstatic delight — in triumphant joy and exultation, to the one only God, our Savior through Jesus Christ our Lord, be glory (splendor), and power and authority, before all time and now and forever — unto all the ages of eternity. Amen — so be it. Jude 24, 25 [Amplified Bible]

READ THESE PASSAGES   IDENTIFICATION IS ...

Colossians 3:3,4
II Peter 1:3, 4
Colossians 1:17
Colossians 2:9
Galatians 2:20
II Corinthians 5:17

_____

_____

Step 1:
Romans 6:1-11
II Corinthians 4:11

_____

_____

Step 2:
John 15:1-17
I John 4:9-21

_____

_____

_____

_____

Step 3:
Galatians 5:16, 24-25
Romans 8:1-17
Romans 12:1,2
Ephesians 5:18

_____

_____

_____

_____

READ THESE PASSAGES   IDENTIFICATION IS ...

Ephesians 1:3- 2:10
        "In Christ ...

_____
_____
_____

        "Power ...

_____
_____
_____

        "Raised ...

_____

        Christ ...

_____
_____
_____

        Us ...

_____
_____

        "Seated ...

_____
_____
_____
_____

READ THESE PASSAGES   GLORIFICATION IS ...

II Thessalonians 1:4-10
John 3:36
Ecclesiastes 12:7
Luke 23:39-43
Acts 7:54-59
II Corinthians 5:6,8
Luke 9:28-36
Genesis 2:7
Genesis 3:1-20
Romans 8:23
I Corinthians 15:12-26
I Corinthians 15:51-58
I Thessalonians 4:13-18
Philippians 3:20,21
I John 3:2
John 20-27,28

_____
_____
_____
_____
_____
_____
_____
_____
_____
_____
_____
_____
_____
_____
_____

These Men Found the Secret

Hudson Taylor

As to work, mine was never so plentiful, so responsible, or so difficult; but the weight and strain are all gone ... When my agony of soul was at its height ... the Spirit of God revealed the truth of our oneness with Jesus as I had never known it before. McCarthy, who had [experienced] the same sense of failure but saw the light before I did, wrote: 'But how to get faith strengthened? Not by striving after faith, but by resting on the Faithful One.'

As I read I saw it all! 'If we believe not, He abideth faithful.' 'Ah, there is rest!' I thought. I have striven in vain to rest in Him. I'll strive no more. For has He not promised to abide with me — never to leave me, never to fail me?

But this was not all He showed me, nor one half. As I thought of the Vine and the Branches, what light the blessed Spirit poured into my soul! How great seemed my mistake in having wished to get the sap, the fullness out of Him. I saw not only that Jesus would never leave me, but that I was a member of His body, of His flesh and of His bones. The vine now I see, is not the root merely, but all — root, stem, branches, twigs, leaves, flowers, fruit; and Jesus is not only that: He is soil and sunshine, air and showers and ten thousand times more than we have ever dreamed, wished for, or needed. Oh, the joy of seeing this truth! I do pray that the eyes of your understanding may be enlightened, that you may know and enjoy the riches freely given us in Christ.

The sweetest part ... is the rest which full identification with Christ brings. I am no longer anxious about anything, as I realize this; for He, I know, is able to carry out His will, and His will is mine.

Francis Schaeffer

Back in 1951 and 1952, I went through a very deep time in my own life. I had been a pastor for ten years and a missionary for another five, and I was connected with a group who stood very strongly for the truth of the Scriptures. But as I watched, it became clear to me that I saw very little spiritual reality. I had to ask why? I looked at myself as well and realized that my own spiritual reality was not as great as it had been immediately after my conversion. We were in Switzerland at the time, and I said to my wife, 'I must really think this through.'

I took about two months, and I walked in the mountains

whenever it was clear. And when it was rainy, I walked back and forth in the hayloft over our chalet. I thought and wrestled and prayed, and I went all the way back to my agnosticism. I asked myself whether I had been right to stop being an agnostic and to become a Christian. I told my wife if it didn't turn out right I was going to be honest and go back to America and put it all aside and do some other work.

I came to realize that indeed I had been right in becoming a Christian. But then I went on further and wrestled deeper and asked, 'But then where is the spiritual reality, Lord among most of that which calls itself orthodoxy?' And gradually I found something. I found something that I had not been taught, a simple thing but profound. I discovered the meaning of the work of Christ, the meaning of the blood of Christ, moment by moment in our lives after we are Christians — the moment-by-moment work of the whole Trinity in our lives because as Christians we are indwelt by the Holy Spirit. This is true spirituality.

Oswald Chambers

God used me during those [previous] years for the conversion of souls, but I had no conscious communion with Him. The Bible was the dullest, most uninteresting book in existence, and the sense of depravity, the vileness and bad-motivedness of my nature, was terrific. I see now that God was taking me by the light of the Holy Spirit and His Word through every ramification of my being....I was getting very desperate. I knew no one who had what I wanted, in fact I did not know what I did want. But I knew that if what I had was all the Christianity there was, the thing was a fraud. Then Luke 11:13 got hold of me...

There are very few crises in life; the great crisis is the surrender of the will. God never crushes a man's will into surrender... He waits until the man yields up his will to Him....'Come unto Me and I will give you rest.' It is after we have begun to experience what salvation means that we surrender our wills to Jesus for rest.... — 'Come unto Me.' It is voluntary coming....'If any man will come after Me, let him deny himself.' The surrender here is of my self to Jesus, my self with His rest at the heart of it. 'If you would be My disciple, give up your right to yourself to Me.' Then the remainder of the life is nothing but the manifestation of this surrender.... It is a question of being united with Jesus in His death until nothing ever appeals to you that did not appeal to Him.... The whole of the life after surrender is an aspiration for unbroken communion with God.

SALVATION

from the **Penalty** of Sin	from the **Power** of Sin	from the **Presence** of Sin

How has your view of salvation been expanded during this study?

_____

_____

_____

Give your thoughts about your freedom from the Penalty of sin.

_____

_____

_____

_____

_____

_____

Give your thoughts about your freedom from the Power of sin.

_____

_____

_____

_____

_____

Give your thoughts about your freedom from the Presence of sin.

_____

_____

_____

_____

_____

Study Number 4

WHAT IS THE BASIS OF ETHICS AND MORALITY?

Does man decide for himself what is right or wrong or is there something outside of man that guides and directs moral decisions? On what grounds does a person decide right from wrong? The answer to these questions is no longer simple. The society in which we live has blurred the dividing line between right and wrong, and in many cases the line between the two no longer exist.

Example 1: Is it right or wrong to have an abortion?
If your answer is that it is wrong to have an abortion, on what basis would you make that moral choice? On the other hand, if your answer is that there is nothing wrong with such a decision, what would be your reason?

Example 2: Is it ever right to lie to someone?
What would your response be? And what reason would you give for the moral choice that you make?

As you can see moral choices are not always easy. Some people in our culture would say that choices can never be placed into a 'right' or 'wrong' category. What does the Bible say about the commands of God?

This is answered in the Psalms:

"[They are] more to be desired...than gold, yea, than much fine gold: sweeter also than honey and the honeycomb. Moreover by them is thy servant warned: and in keeping of them there is great reward. Who can understand his errors? Cleanse thou me from secret faults. Keep back thy servant also from presumptuous sins; let them not have dominion over me: then shall I be upright, and I shall be innocent from the great transgression."

Character of God	Commands of God	Consequences
Matthew 5:48	Psalms 19:7a	
John 8:25-30	Psalms 19:7b	
Deuteronomy 32:4	Psalms 19:8a	
John 1:1-9; 8:12; 12:45	Psalms 19:8b	
Ezra 9:15; Job 4:17; I John .2:1	Psalms 19: 9	

We live in a universe created by a moral God. He has expressed Himself through the laws and moral principles found in Scripture. Because His word is the exact expression of His character, God Himself is therefore the standard. We know that Jesus is the exact radiance and perfect expression of God (Hebrews 1:3). "In the beginning was the Word … and the Word became flesh and dwelt among us" (John 1:1, 14). We live in a moral universe, made known to us through the prophets and ultimately through His Son, with absolutes by which we can know right from wrong.

Although the law of God is perfect because God is perfect, what was the weakness of the law? Read Hebrews 7:18, 19.

Was the problem with the law?
Read Romans 8: 1-7.

Read Hebrews 10
The law is said to be ...

This Man (Jesus) is said to be ...

Jesus was able to do what the law was unable to do.
What was that?

Read II Corinthians 5:17, Philippians 2:13, and II Peter 1:4.
Describe our new life in Christ.

_____

_____

_____

The commands of the Lord are the reflection of the very nature and character of God. Since the commands of God issue forth from God, it is only reasonable to understand them to reveal His character. Collectively the commandments instruct us as to what choices are right and protect us from making choices that are wrong. Therefore the basis of ethics and morality rest not upon the personal preferences of culture, but rather upon the very nature and character of God Himself.

The beauty of Christianity is that it is not simply a rule of thumb to live by. We are able to express the character of God in our own lives not through grim determination, but because the Spirit of God indwells us. As we live moment-by-moment in surrender to Him, He then reproduces His life in and through us resulting in love, joy, peace, patience, kindness, goodness, faithfulness, gentleness, and self-control (Galatians 5:22, 23).

How would you respond to someone who said that each person must decide for himself what is right and what is wrong?

_____
_____
_____
_____
_____
_____
_____
_____
_____
_____
_____
_____
_____

Is Christianity simply a code of ethics to live by or is there something more? What provision has God made for a person to live a life that reflects the nature and character of God?

_____
_____
_____
_____
_____
_____
_____
_____
_____
_____
_____
_____
_____
_____
_____
_____

WHAT IS THE CAUSE OF EVIL AND SUFFERING?

"Do I serve God for nothing?"
"I just don't understand! Why did this happen to me?"
"Either God must not be all-good or He is not all-powerful."
"If God created the world, where did all the ugliness come from?"
"How could a good God exist in light of all the misery in the world?"

Throughout all history, man has struggled with the problem of evil and suffering. Though there are not simple answers to these questions, the Bible does give a sense of understanding.

READ THESE PASSAGES   HOW IS GOD DESCRIBED IN THESE PASSAGES?

Psalms 25:8 _____
Psalms 33:5 _____
Psalms 34:8 _____
Psalms 119:68 _____
Psalms 145:7 _____
Isaiah 63:7 _____
Jeremiah 33:11 _____
Nahum 1:7 _____
Matthew 19:17 _____
Romans 2:4 _____
Romans 11:22 _____

Genesis 1 - 2:1 Circle or underline the description that God gives regarding what He created.

The Creation was ... _____

The Creation of man was ... _____

Is God the source of evil? _____

Since God is all-good, and what He created was described as 'very good', then the source of evil is not in God.

God saw everything that He had created and He described it as 'very good' (Genesis 1:31). Man was created to have a loving relationship with God. Did God create man as a robot without the ability to make moral choices, or is he a free moral agent? Why is this an important question?

READ THESE PASSAGES   HOW IS MAN DESCRIBED?

Genesis 2:15 - 17;   _____
Jeremiah 35:15   _____
Ezekiel 33:11   _____
Hosea 6:1   _____
Matthew 22:3   _____
Luke 14:17   _____
II Corinthians 5:20   _____
Revelation 3:20   _____

Circle the kind of being man is ...

Robot   Free Moral Agent

What did man choose? And what was the result?
Genesis 3:16-19   _____
Isaiah 43:27   _____
Romans 5:8 - 21   _____
I Corinthians 15:21   _____
I Timothy 2:14-15   _____

What is the Christians view of the source of evil?

_____
_____
_____
_____

Evil entered into our world through the choice of Adam. It was Eve, of course, who was deceived by Satan.

You may ask: "Does God have enough power to stop evil?"

Job 42:2 _____
Psalms 115:3 _____
Psalms 135:6 _____
Isaiah 43:13 _____
Habakkuk 3:6 _____
Matthew 19:26 _____
Mark 14:36 _____
Luke 1:37 _____
Revelation 19:6 _____

"Then why doesn't God destroy evil?"

II Peter 3:3 - 13 _____
Genesis 6 and 7 _____
Lamentations 3:22 _____
Ezekiel 33:11 _____

In the past what has God done concerning evil?

What is He going to do in the future?

Why does God not destroy all evil right now?

What has God done about evil?

II Corinthians 5:21 _____
Isaiah 53:12 _____
Psalms 69:20, 21 _____
Romans 5:8 _____
Luke 19:41 _____

READ THESE PASSAGES   WHAT IS THE CHRISTIAN'S VIEW OF SUFFERING?

Job 42:5,6
II Corinthians 1:9
_____
_____

Hebrews 12:5,6
_____
_____

II Corinthians 12:7 - 10
_____
_____

I Peter 1:6,7
Hebrews 3:17, 18
_____
_____
_____

James 1:4
_____
_____

I Peter 4:12, 13
_____
_____

Philippians 3:10, 11
_____
_____

I Corinthians 11:20-32
_____
_____
_____

I Peter 5:10
_____
_____

John 9:3
_____

Write a letter to someone who is or has experienced suffering in their own life. Use the space below to summarize your thoughts.

_____
_____
_____
_____
_____
_____
_____
_____
_____
_____
_____
_____
_____
_____

WHAT HAPPENS TO MAN AT DEATH?

What happens to man at death? Does man simply cease to exist, does he wait to return to earth in some other form, or does he go into some other world? The answer a person gives to these and other similar questions is very personal and usually evokes strong emotions. For our answer let us turn to Jesus as He pulls back the curtain of eternity for us to have a glimpse.

Read Luke 16:19-31.
Describe the …
Rich Man (19)   Lazarus (20, 21)

Jesus says that both men died (22).
What happened to each man at death?

Describe the…
Rich man's condition in hell.   Lazarus' condition.

How does Abraham respond to the rich man?

What is the relationship between heaven and hell?
What do we learn about 'moving' between heaven and hell?

How did Jesus answer the question:
'What Happens to Man at Death?"

Death is either the door to life with God and his people or the door to eternal separation from God who is the only one that can bring ultimate fulfillment and meaning to life.

HEAVEN
READ THESE PASSAGES   HEAVEN IS THE PLACE OF ...

PSALMS 33:13, 14   _____
MATTHEW 6:9   _____
ACTS 1:11   _____

JOHN 14: 1-3   _____
JOHN 17: 5, 24   _____
I THESSALONIANS 4:16, 17 _____

II CORINTHIANS 12:2, 4   _____
II CORINTHIANS 5:1-8   _____

PSALMS 23:6   _____
REVELATION 21:4   _____

REVELATION 5:6   _____
REVELATION 14:1   _____
REVELATION 22:4   _____

JEREMIAH 30:22   _____
EPHESIANS 2:7   _____
EPHESIANS 3:9   _____
I CORINTHIANS 2:9   _____

Hell

Read These Passages	What Do We Learn About Hell?
Matthew 25:41-46	_____
Revelation 20:11-15	_____

_____
_____
_____
_____

Read These Passages	How is Hell Described?
Jude 7, 13	_____
Matthew 8:12	_____
Matthew 13: 42, 50	_____
Matthew 22:13	_____
Matthew 24:51	_____
Matthew 25:30	_____
II Thessalonians 1:7-9	_____
II Peter 3:7	_____
I Thessalonians 5:3	_____
Revelations 20:10	_____
Luke 16:23	_____

Read These Passages	What is Taught About The Resurrection?
Psalms 49:15	_____
Psalms 71:20	_____
Hosea 13:14	_____
John 5:25	_____
John 6:40	_____
John 11:25	_____
Acts 24:15	_____
I Corinthians 15:22	_____
II Corinthians 4:14	_____
I Thessalonians 4:16	_____

This discussion will be continued in the next section.

What happens to man at death? Does man simply cease to exist, does he wait to return to earth in some other form, or does he go into some other world? What is your answer to this question?

_____

_____

_____

_____

_____

_____

_____

_____

_____

_____

_____

_____

_____

_____

_____

_____

_____

_____

_____

_____

_____

_____

_____

_____

_____

_____

_____

_____

_____

_____

_____

_____

Study Number 7

WHAT IS THE MEANING OF HISTORY?

What is going to happen next?

"The world is not going to get better and better. The Christian's hope is not the gradual betterment of the world, but that Christ is coming back again."

Dr. Francis Schaeffer

READ THESE PASSAGES   WHAT IS GOING TO HAPPEN NEXT?

Luke 17:26-30   _____
Luke 18:8   _____

Acts 1:10,11   _____
Mark 13:26   _____
I Corinthians 15:23   _____
Philippians 3:20,21   _____
I Thessalonians 1:10   _____
I Thessalonians 2:19   _____
I Thessalonians 3:13   _____
I Thessalonians 4:14,16,17 _____
II Thessalonians 1:7   _____
I Timothy 6:14   _____
Titus 2:12,13   _____
II Peter 3:3-14   _____
Revelation 1:7,8   _____

Acts 1:6-9   _____
Matthew 24:36   _____
Matthew 25:13   _____
Mark 13:32,33   _____
Luke 12:35-40   _____

I Thessalonians 3:13   _____
I Thessalonians 4:13-17   _____

Matthew 24:36-44   _____
Luke 17:26-30, 34-36   _____
Isaiah 26:19-21   _____

Matthew 25:1-13   _____
                                    _____

II Thessalonians 2:1-12   _____
Revelation 13:1-18   _____

Revelation 6:1-17   _____
Revelation 8:7-9:2   _____
Revelation 11:13, 14   _____
Revelation 15:1   _____

Revelation 16:13-16   _____
Revelation 19: 11-21   _____

Revelation 20:1-6   _____
Romans 8:18-23   _____
Isaiah 11:1-10   _____

Revelation 20:6   _____
Luke 19:11-27   _____

Romans 11:25-29   _____
Isaiah 11:10-12:6   _____
Jeremiah 30:7-11   _____
Zechariah 12:8-10   _____
Zechariah 13:6   _____
Zechariah 14:16-21   _____

Revelation 20:7-15   _____

Revelation 21:1-22:5   _____

What is going to happen next in history?
What is the Christians' hope? Describe where history is going.

_____

_____

_____

_____

_____

_____

_____

_____

_____

Make a time -line illustrating the Christian view of history.
Show what is going to happen in the future.

_____

"Our understanding of Nature, and our interpretation of History, are both partial and faulty; yet, if we are Christians at all, we must believe that back of both is the Divine Thinker, the Infinite Wisdom, and the Almighty Power, Who is the Son of God our Redeemer and Life.

"Things have not been started and then left to run on their own material or moral momentum, but all things are under the constant control of the Divine Creator, in Whom all things have their center of unity, Who appoints to everything its place, Who combines all into an ordered whole, so that this Universe is a cosmos and not chaos.

"It is not law ultimately which rules this Universe, but God our Father, and He rules it through His Son our Saviour. Human history is not in the grip of fate, but in the hands of Him Who was pierced for us on Calvary."

Dr. Wm. Graham Scroggie

OTHER MATERIALS BY DAVID QUINE

Let Us Highly Resolve

David and Shirley Quine's twenty one years of experience raising and educating their nine children are condensed here in an immensely practical, real and profound book for today's Christian parents. In addition to discipling their own children, the Quines are committed to encouraging and leading other families to this high calling.

128 page soft cover book
$10.00.

World Views of the Western World

The three volume research-teaching syllabus assists you in making a personal analysis of the significant thoughts and ideas that have shaped the significant moments in western history.

Volume 1, 638 page soft bound book
$125.00

Volume 2, 650 page soft bound book
$125.00

Volume 3, a future publication

For information regarding other materials written by David Quine request:

The Cornerstone Catalog

The Cornerstone Curriculum Project
2006 Flat Creek Place
Richardson, Texas 75080
(972) 235-5149